Percussion Guide for the Beginning Band Student

By Nick Backos

A focus on sound quality for percussion instruments

*Cover photograph, book layout and design
by Nick Backos
Cover inspired by Lisa Lockhart*

Contributing Editors:
*Bruce Albright, Dawn Badger and
John Robertson*

Percussion Guide for the Beginning Band Student

Nick Backos Publications LLC
Saint Clair Shores, MI. 48081
nickbackos.com
email: nickbackos@gmail.com

Copyright © 2008, by Nick Backos
All rights reserved.

No portion of this book may be reproduced in any form without the
prior written permission of the publisher.

ISBN 978-0-615-32108-0

Dedications

This book is dedicated to all music educators who have given their time and talent in inspiring thousands of students in fulfilling their personal dreams through music.

Acknowledgments

There are many people I would like thank for their encouragement over the years: My parents George and Mary Backos for their encouragement in my quest to fulfill my carrier in music; My son Troy who makes me a proud father, my brother Dean, sister in-law Kim, Megan and Mathew for their support. To my extended family, aunts, uncles and cousins, thank you for your support. Special thanks to my uncle, Bob Samaras, educator, author, and coach, for his constant encouragement and advice.

My many private instructors: Salvatore Rabbio, Mark Logsdon, Dave Hunt, Sam Tunda, Keith Claeys, Michael Zelenak, Danny Spencer, Matt Michaels, Rob Pipho, Bill Gaff, and Jan Albright. My past band and orchestra directors: Bill Berndt, Ron Cardeccia, Harold Arnoldi, and Valter Poole. Thanks to my talented colleagues and friends from Avondale Public Schools and Macomb Community College for their support in giving me a creative working environment. Thanks to my talented fellow musicians who I have performed with for so many years who keep me learning and playing.

Special thanks to my following friends who read through this guide with editing and comments: Bruce Albright, Dawn Badger, John Robertson, Norm Euker, Shari Krishnan and Bethany Widmer.

Finally, thanks to all of the many students I have had the privilege of teaching in my career. You have truly been an inspiration for this book.

About The Author

Nick Backos is a professional musician and educator in the greater Detroit area. He is a retired band director who taught for the Avondale School District for over 25 years and is currently a private percussion instructor at Macomb Community College. His schedule is busy not only as an educator, but also as a performer in classical and jazz music. Currently, Nick splits his time between timpanist for the Macomb Symphony Orchestra, Grosse Pointe Symphony Orchestra and drum set for the Rhythm Society Orchestra, a 15 piece swing big band. He is also a freelance percussionist in all styles of music.

Nick has been a featured soloist performing *The Golden Age of the Xylophone*, arranged by Floyd Werle and Randall Eyles, and Darius Milhaud's *Concerto for Percussion and Small Orchestra*. He is a graduate from Wayne State University with bachelor degrees in performance and music education; master's degree in information and library science and a master's certificate in orchestral studies. Also, he received a certification in music technology from Berklee College of Music.

Directors Notes

I have been a band director for over 25 years and a professional percussionist even longer. To this day I am amazed how difficult it has been to develop an organized, knowledgeable and cohesive percussion section due to class size and time limitations. Every band director spends numerous hours developing a characteristic tone for each instrument. Developing tone quality must be taught to the percussion section at the earliest stage.

In a rehearsal, I would hear evidence of the many problems a young percussionist was having in handling the variety of instruments. My frustration was the inability to give the time and explanation needed for a percussionist to remember this enormous amount of information. A misconception about the percussion section is how easy it is to play these instruments. In reality, it is easy to get a sound on an instrument, but difficult to get a quality, characteristic sound. This instruction book was developed to help solve this problem.

This book is structured for the beginning percussionist in a straightforward, organized design, and it will give band directors a tool for saving time in developing a polished percussion section. Understanding that there are a variety of grips, mallets and instruments to choose from, I focused on the most common instruments and techniques. Through these lessons, students can develop fundamental skills and concepts to expand on as they develop. This method book with its consistent design, study guide, pictorial section, and assessment, will give your students the ability to achieve the unique distinction of becoming a percussionist.

The Structure of this Book

Percussion Guide for the Beginning Band Student is designed so students can complete a lesson in 5 to 10 minutes of class time. It is important for the band director to introduce the lesson before students begin the assignment. Then, while a conductor is working with a different section or possibly band warm ups, the percussion section can be engaged in their daily or weekly lesson.

<u>Each lesson has four sections.</u>
- Description of the instrument.
- Key points – no more than seven per lesson.
- Questions to help reinforce key points.
- The Art of Imitation – pictorial view through the eyes of a percussionist.

Practice Tips

- Take your time on each lesson and make sure to answer every question. Even if you feel a lesson is easy or that you really know the material, do not rush through to the next lesson. There are many new concepts to remember so allow time for each *key point* to be part of your technique.

- If you are having trouble remembering the *key points* and answering the questions, then look at the IMITATE WHAT YOU SEE section and then answer the questions.

- The basic rule for all percussionists is that the position of your fingers, hands, and body will dictate the sound of the instrument. Before you play a note, review the *key points* regarding grip, body position, and striking technique.

- Practice in front of a mirror to visualize the proper techniques.

- All great musicians play with a great sound so always <u>LISTEN, LISTEN, AND LISTEN</u>! Remember this simple rule: If the sound is pleasing to your ear, you are on the right track. Remember to play the drum, not pound the drum.

- Always approach music with a positive attitude. Your enthusiasm will show up in how you play!

Contents

Lesson One
Sticks and Mallets – page 8
Stick Bag and Supplies – page 9

Lesson Two
Music Stand – page 10
Imitate What You See – page 11

Lesson Three
Legato and Staccato
Instruments – page 12

Lesson Four
Match Grip – page 14
Imitate What You See – page 15

Lesson Five
Match Grip Variations – page 16
Imitate What You See – page 17

Lesson Six
Dynamics/Heights of Sticks – page 18
Imitate What You See – page 19

Lesson Seven
Developing Tone Quality – page 20

Lesson Eight
Snare Drum - page 22
Imitate What You See – page 23

Lesson Nine
Bass Drum – page 24
Imitate What You See – page 25

Lesson Ten
Suspended Cymbal – page 26
Imitate What You See – page 27

Eleven Lesson
Crash Cymbals – page 28
Imitate What You See – page 29

Lesson Twelve
Triangle – page 30
Imitate What You See – page 31

Lesson Thirteen
Tambourine – page 32
Imitate What You See – page 33

Lesson Fourteen
Claves – page 34
Imitate What You See – page 35

Lesson Fifteen
Maracas – page 36
Imitate What You See – page 37

Lesson Sixteen
Cowbell – page 38
Imitate What You See – page 39

Lesson Seventeen
Temple Blocks – page 40
Imitate What You See – page 41

Lesson Eighteen A
Mallet Instruments – page 42
Mallet Choice - page 43

Lesson Eighteen B
Mallets Instruments – page 44
Imitate What You See – page 45

Lesson Nineteen A
Timpani – page 46
Imitate What You See – page 47

Lesson Nineteen B
Timpani Tuning – page 48

Lesson One
Sticks and Mallets

Description

As a percussionist, there are many sticks and mallets you can choose from. Listed below is a set of sticks and mallets that will take care of many situations needed in playing classical music. This list is only a starting point and a guide for buying additional mallets as the situation dictates. As far as brands, it is an individual choice.

Key Points

- **Stick Bag** - It is always wise to buy a stick bag when buying your first sticks. These bags are designed to hold a variety of mallets and sticks in a simple carrying bag. This will keep you from losing your equipment. The bag does not have to be fancy or expensive, but it is an important item.

- **Snare Sticks** - Any 5A or 5B drum sticks. The higher the number the thinner the drumsticks, so a 7A stick is thinner than a 5A stick. Also, the letter (A) refers to a thinner stick than the letter (B) stick. If in doubt, ask the percussion specialist at your local music store to help you with your decision.

- **Yarn Mallets (medium hard)** - One set of yarn mallets can be used for marimba, vibraphone, and suspended cymbal rolls.

- **Xylophone/Bell Mallets** – There are two types of mallets that will work for both bells and xylophone. These mallets are made of acrylic and hard rubber.

- **Timpani Mallets** – Timpani mallets are covered with felt. Start with a general or staccato timpani mallet. Either mallet will work.

Questions

1. What drum stick size is recommended for snare drum, 5A or 7A?
   _____
2. Name two types of mallets used for xylophone and bells.
   _____
3. What type of mallet is recommended for marimba?
   _____
4. Name one type of timpani mallet you should purchase.
   _____

STICK BAG AND SUPPLIES

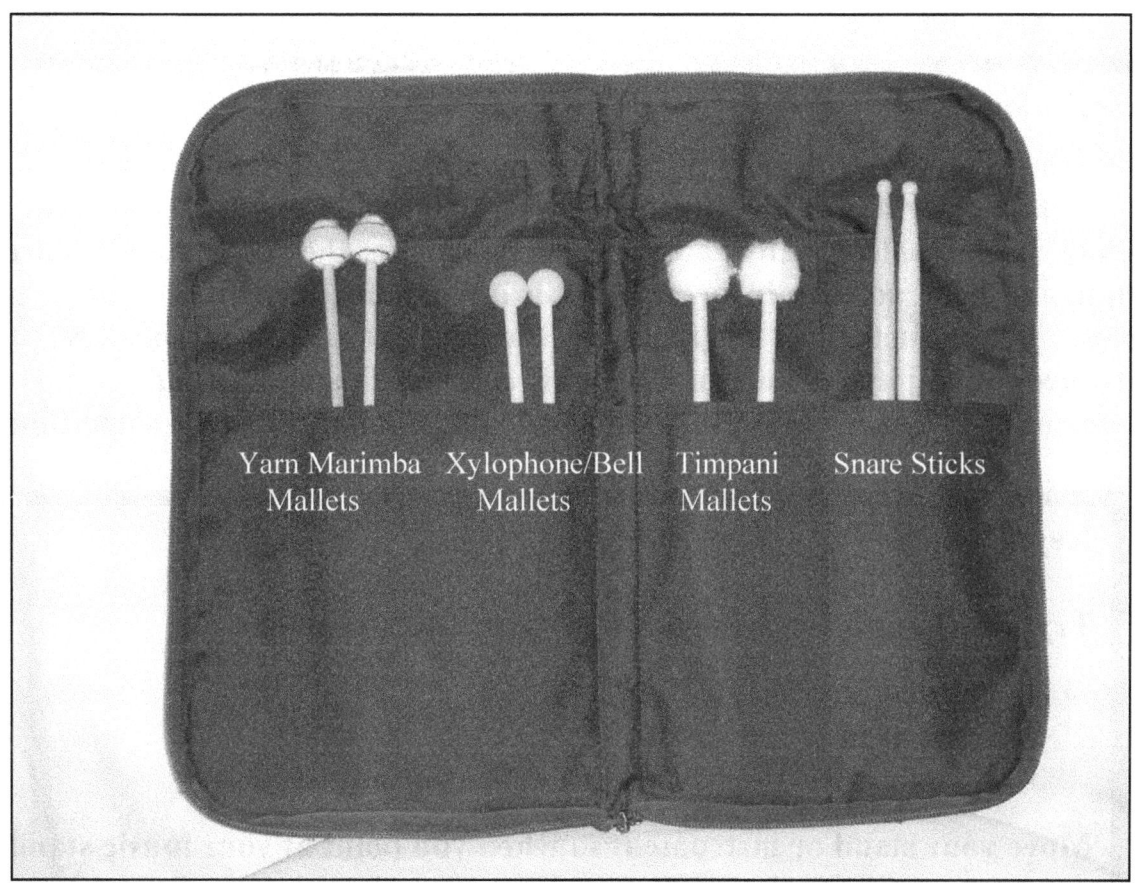

PERCUSSION CHECK LIST
(Check supplies that you have.)

- **Stick Bag** _____
- **Yarn Marimba Mallets** _____
- **Xylophone/Bell Mallets** _____
- **Timpani Mallets** _____
- **Snare Sticks** _____

Lesson Two
Music Stand

Description

This simple piece of equipment can cause you many problems that will affect your total performance. Finding the correct height and angle is important in feeling comfortable. Many young percussionists set the music stand, snare drum, and body position incorrectly. It is important to see the conductor at all times. The conductor will be giving musical cues such as the tempo, key entrances of major sections, and dynamic changes throughout the performance. Your goal is to see the music and conductor at the same time.

Key Points

Try this simple exercise and it will correct this problem.

1. Point at your music stand.
2. Point at the conductor.
3. If you moved your arm, then make this adjustment:

Move your stand or instrument so when you point at your music stand, you are pointing at the conductor. Your arm should not move.

(USE THIS TECHNIQUE FOR ALL PERCUSSION INSTRUMENTS.)

Questions

1. What adjustments should you make if you can't see the conductor while you are playing?
   _____
   _____

2. Why is it important to see the conductor?
   _____
   _____

IMITATE WHAT YOU SEE

Point at the music stand.
Point at the conductor.
Adjust the snare and music stand if needed.

Lesson Three
Legato and Staccato Percussion Instruments

Description

It is important for you to be able to distinguish percussion instruments in two categories: *legato* and *staccato* instruments.

- *Legato* means the notes are long and sustained. *Legato* instruments need to be muffled when clarity or measures of silence are called for.

- *Staccato* means the notes are short and detached. Many staccato instruments need to be sustained to create length of sound. This is why the classical drum roll, known as the *buzz roll,* is used for the snare drum.

    REMEMBER: <u>LEGATO</u> – LONG, <u>STACCATO</u> – SHORT

Key Points

Legato Percussion Instruments
- Bass Drum
- Timpani
- Bells
- Triangle
- Cymbals

Staccato Percussion Instruments
- Snare Drum
- Tom Toms
- Xylophone
- Marimba
- Temple Blocks
- Claves

Questions

Write the letter (S) by all *staccato* instruments and the letter (L) by all the *legato* instruments.

1. Snare Drum _____
2. Bass Drum _____
3. Cymbals _____
4. Timpani _____
5. Claves _____
6. Tom Toms _____
7. Temple Blocks _____
8. Bells _____
9. Xylophone _____
10. Triangle _____
11. Marimba _____

REMINDER

ALWAYS REVIEW PREVIOUS LESSONS

Lesson Four
Match Grip

Description

There are two types of snare drum grips, the traditional grip and the match grip. These grips are a way of holding the drum sticks. I recommend as a beginning percussionist you use the match grip. Even though many percussionists use both grips, this grip will give you a natural feel compared to the traditional grip. The match grip can be used for every instrument and for every style of music.

Key Points

- **The stick is held between the first finger and the thumb (known as the *fulcrum*) and the other fingers wrap gently around the stick.**
- **The fulcrum is the pressure point that holds the stick.**
- **The stick is held approximately 5 inches from the back of the stick.**
- **The stick should be held loosely to create maximum vibration on the stick but always maintain the fulcrum.**
- **Both hands holding the stick should look identical which gives the name "match grip".**
- **When playing, use only your wrist without using your arm to develop the correct muscle group.**

Questions

1. What two fingers grip the stick?
   _____
2. Do you hold the stick tightly or loosely?
   _____
3. Define "fulcrum"?
   _____
4. When playing, do you use your arm or wrist?
   _____
5. What is the name of the grip you have learned and why is the name given to this grip?
   _____

IMITATE WHAT YOU SEE

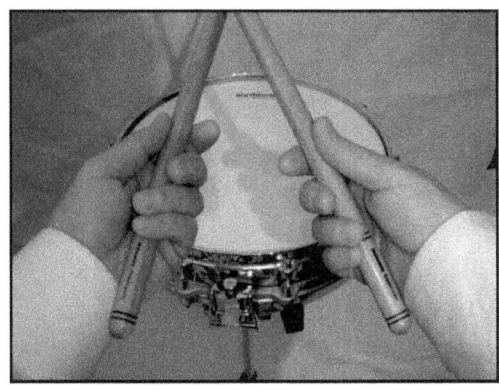

*Look at your left hand and right hand.
They should look identical. Then turn wrist.*

Place tip of sticks close together.

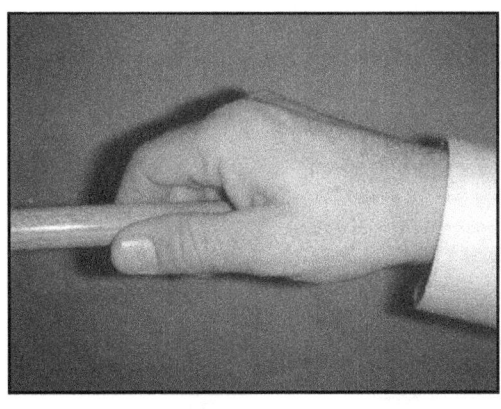

Don't hold the stick tight. Notice a slight opening in your hands

Lesson Five
Match Grip Variations
French, American, and German Grip

Description

There are three variations of the match grip that you need to know. All three variations can be used on a variety of instruments. I am giving you some common rules for each grip. The angle of your hands determines the grip. Pay close attention to the" Imitate What You See" section.

Key Points

- *French Grip* creates the lightest sounding tone. This is the common grip when playing the timpani. Your thumb will be located on the top of the stick.

- *American Grip* creates a medium sounding tone. This is the common grip used for snare drum and mallet instruments. Your hands will turn inward, with your thumb on the side of the stick, to create a slight angle. <u>This is the most natural grip and truly can be used on all instruments for a beginning percussionist.</u>

- *German Grip* creates the heaviest, darkest sounding tone. This grip can be used on timpani and as a starting point for mallet instruments. The palm of your hand is flat, facing the floor, parallel to the ground which puts more weight and pressure into the timpani head.

Questions

1. Which is the most common grip when playing snare drum?_____
2. Which is the most common grip when playing timpani? _____
3. Which two grips can you use when playing mallets? _____
4. Which grip can a beginning percussionist use for all percussion instruments?_____

IMITATE WHAT YOU SEE

FRENCH GRIP – *Thumb is on top of stick.*

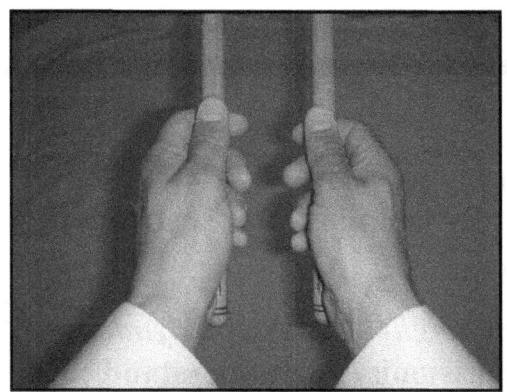
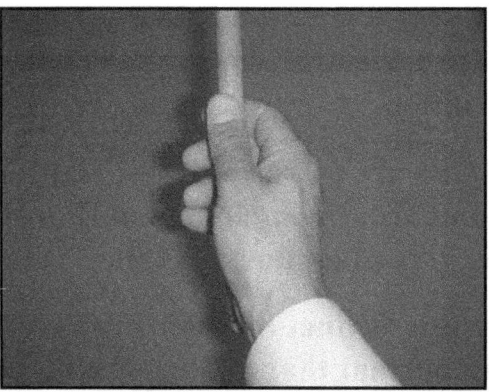

AMERICAN GRIP – *Slightly angle hands inward.*

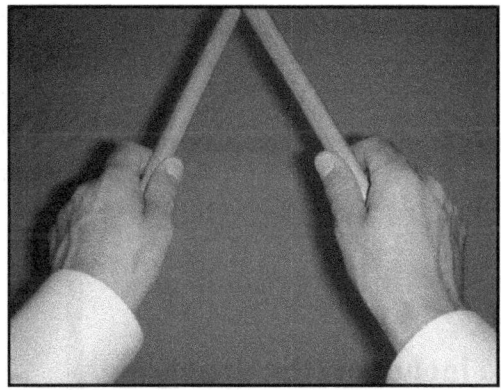
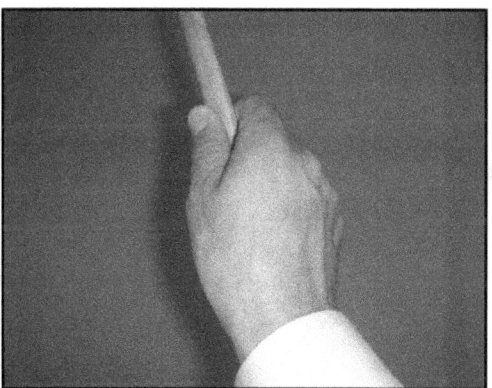

GERMAN GRIP – *Palm of hand is parallel to the ground.*

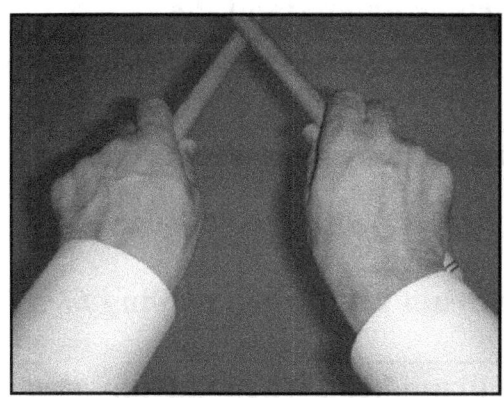
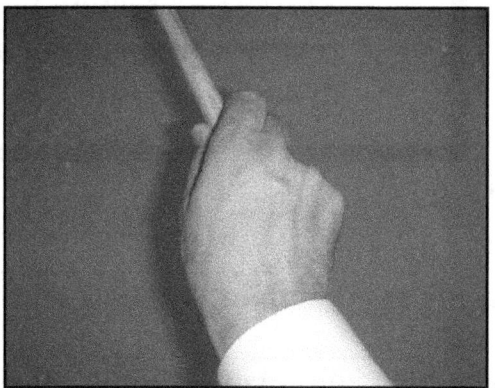

Lesson Six
Dynamics/Height of Stick

Description

Dynamics are extremely important in playing percussion instruments. *Dynamics* means how loudly you play your instrument. The degree of loudness is called volume.

There is a distinct relationship between *height of stick* and *dynamics*. It is important that as a beginning percussionist you understand this concept. This will keep you from over playing (playing too loud) in band.

Height of Stick is the best technique to use to control dynamics. It is also the easiest to begin with.

Key Points

- Tips of sticks are five inches off the drum head when playing *forte* (loud).
- Tips of the sticks are two inches off the drum head when playing *piano* (soft).
- Pay close attention to the "IMITATE WHAT YOU SEE" section to further understand the relationship between height of stick and dynamics.

Questions

1. Define dynamics. _____
2. How high is the tip of the stick off the drum head when playing *forte* (loud)? _____
3. How high is the tip of the stick off the drum head when playing *piano* (soft)? _____

IMITATE WHAT YOU SEE

Loud (forte) - Tip of stick is five inches off the drum head.

Soft (piano) - Tip of stick is two inches off the drum head.

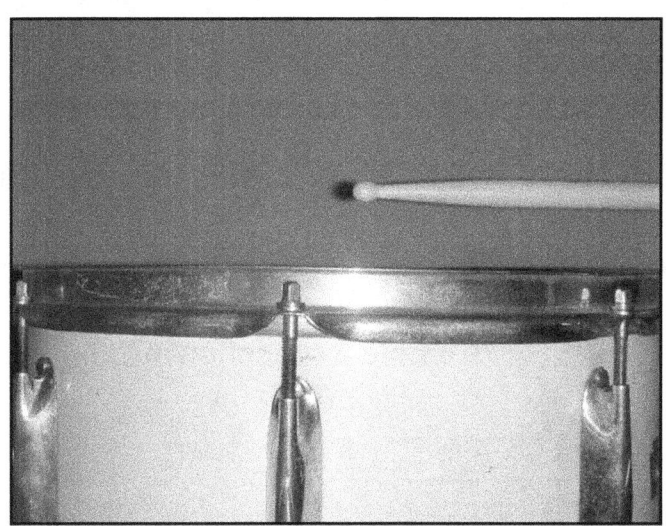

Lesson Seven

DEVELOPING TONE QUALITY
FOUR RULES TO REMEMBER

Description

Tone quality is the sound of an instrument. All great musicians have one common quality: they have a great sound on their musical instrument. Qualities of tone can be described as warm, rich, or a full body sound that is characteristic of the instrument. A beginning musician should ask one question: <u>*is my tone pleasing to the ear*</u>?

Key Points

FOUR TECHNIQUES THAT WILL IMPROVE TONE QUALITY

- **RELAX YOUR HANDS** – Never hold the sticks tight but maintain the <u>fulcrum</u> for stick control; let the sticks vibrate in your hands. This will allow the stick to naturally strike the drum head. *It should feel like gravity is pulling the stick to the drum head without the wrist interfering with the motion.*

- **USE ONLY THE WRIST-** *Many percussionists use their arm in combination with a wrist stroke. A young percussionist needs to develop the correct muscle group before adding arm to their technique.* As a beginning percussionist, focus on using your wrist.

- **USE HEIGHT OF STICK** for controlling dynamics.

- **LET THE STICK BOUNCE** off the drum head. Think of pulling the sound out of the drum.

Questions

Complete the following statement.

1. Relax _____
2. Use only _____
3. Height of _____
4. Let the stick _____
5. You should ask yourself: is my tone _____ to my ear?

REMINDER

ALWAYS REVIEW PREVIOUS LESSONS

Lesson Eight
Snare Drum

Description

The snare drum is one of the most popular instruments in the percussion section. It is a two-headed drum with snares stretched along the bottom head. The wire snares give this drum its name and unique sound. It is a staccato instrument, making a sound of short duration. To sustain sound, you will play a classical drum roll (also called the "buzz roll"). As a percussionist you must focus on rhythmic clarity and accuracy when playing the snare drum.

Key Points

Drum alignment
- Keep the snare drum flat like the surface of a table.
- Keep the <u>throw-off</u> (lever that lifts up and down the snares) directly in front of you. This allows you to play over the wire snares for rhythmic clarity.
- Height of the snare should be belt level. *A snare drum too high uses too much bounce and a snare drum too low uses too much wrist.*
- Place the tips of the sticks close together, slightly off center on the drum head. This will create an even sound between your left and right sticks.

Dos and Don'ts
- In band, use classical drum sticks only. Do not use them on a drum set because playing excessive rim shots will wear out your sticks.
- Never play on the thin bottom head of a snare drum with your drum sticks. You will damage the head.
- **Reminder – <u>Relax hands, use only wrist, height of stick, and let sticks bounce.</u>**

Questions

1. What angle should you have the snare drum? _____
2. What is the <u>throw-off</u> on a snare drum for? _____
3. Should the <u>throw-off</u> be in front or on the side of the snare drum? _____
4. How high should you raise the snare drum? _____
5. Should you use your classical drum sticks when playing on a drum set? _____
6. Should the tips of the snare sticks be far apart or close together? _____

IMITATE WHAT YOU SEE

The snare drum is flat and the throw-off is directly in front of you.

Place tip of the sticks close together, slightly off center on the drum head.

Lesson Nine
Bass Drum

Description

The bass drum is the largest of all the percussion instruments. It is a two-headed drum that produces a low resonant sound. Many times the bass drum player has the most responsibility. The low range of this instrument creates a full ensemble sound that makes this instrument incredibly important. It is a *legato* instrument, so muffling (dampening) is needed for sound control and clarity.

Key Points

- Hold the bass drum mallet with your right hand. The beating spot is <u>off center</u> on the drum head.
- To lightly dampen the bass drum, keep your left hand fingertips on the drum head.
- To heavily dampen the bass drum, keep your entire hand on the bass drum.
- The bass drum mallet is heavy. Use mainly <u>wrist</u>, with slight <u>arm</u> motion when playing.
- Use only the bass drum mallet, never drum sticks.
- Never play into the bass drum head which will create a pounding sound. Let the bass drum mallet bounce off the drum head. Think of pulling the sound out of the head.

Questions

1. What hand holds the bass drum mallet? _____
2. Why do you keep your left hand on the bass drum head? _____
_____
3. Should you play the bass drum near the center or off center on the head? _____
4. Should you use your wrist and arm when playing?
_____
5. Should you play into the bass drum head or think of pulling the sound out of the head? _____
6. Should you use a drum stick on a bass drum? _____

IMITATE WHAT YOU SEE

The black dot (off center) is the beating spot for the bass drum mallet.

Leave your left hand on the white dot to slightly muffle the bass drum.

Lesson Ten
Suspended Cymbal

Description

The Suspended Cymbal is a crash cymbal suspended on a cymbal stand. You strike it with a stick or mallet depending on the musical situation. It is used in a variety of situations, from playing rhythms to creating the unique effect of a cymbal roll. The suspended cymbal is a *legato* instrument and at times needs to be muffled.

Key Points

- When playing rhythms on a suspended cymbal, use a drum stick. <u>Always play rhythms with the tip of the stick, not the side (*shaft*) of the stick.</u>
- If the ring of the cymbal interferes with the rhythm you are playing, slightly hold the cymbal with your left hand for rhythmic clarity.
- To create the sound of crash cymbals (*cymbal crash*), <u>strike the cymbal with the *shaft* of the drum stick.</u>
- Use yarn mallets for cymbal rolls, keep mallets apart when playing a roll.
- Locate the *bell* of the cymbal. (see photo) Striking the *bell* can create a cowbell sound.
- Muffle the cymbal after playing a rhythmic section in measures of silence.

Questions

1. Do you use sticks or mallets when playing a cymbal roll? _____
2. Do you use sticks or mallets when playing rhythm? _____
3. When do you muffle the cymbal? _____
4. When making a cymbal sound like a cowbell, what part of the cymbal do you play? _____
5. How do you create a *cymbal crash*? _____

IMITATE WHAT YOU SEE

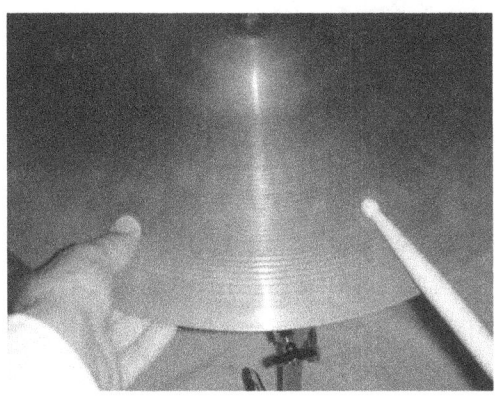

Use the <u>tip of the stick</u> to play rhythm.
Use the <u>shaft of the stick</u> to create a cymbal crash.
Left hand is used to muffle the cymbal when needed.

Use yarn mallets when playing a cymbal roll. Keep mallets apart.

To create a cowbell sound, strike the bell of the cymbal with the shaft of a drum stick.

Lesson Eleven
Crash Cymbals

Description

The crash cymbals are a pair of suspended cymbals held one in each hand, struck together to create a loud, sharp sound. Most students want to play this instrument, but you may find the heavy weight of the crash cymbals makes it extremely uncomfortable. There are advanced techniques in playing crash cymbals but I will give you a simple, effective approach known as the *"One Handed Technique"*. Pay close attention to the proper way to pick up and hold crash cymbals.

Key Points

- Holding crash cymbals can be confusing. Try this technique:
    1. Place cymbals on the floor.
    2. Pick up cymbals. Your thumb and index finger will almost touch the cymbals.
    3. Hold cymbals straight and together. They will look identical. Now, separate cymbals. (See Photo)
    4. Tilt the top edge of the right cymbal slightly towards the left cymbal; hold the left cymbal still and <u>crash the right cymbal into it in an upward motion.</u>
- Crash Cymbals are a *legato* instrument. When needed, muffle cymbals against your body.
- Place the cymbals on a <u>trap table</u> to rest your hands and arms when not playing. (See Photo)

Questions

1. Which hand (cymbal) do you move when striking a cymbal? _____
2. How do you muffle crash cymbals? _____
3. In measures of silence, how do you rest your hands and arms while holding the cymbals? _____

INITATE WHAT YOU SEE

The One Handed Technique

Pick up the cymbals off the ground.

Notice your thumb and index finger almost touches the cymbal. Your left hand is identical to your right hand when holding the cymbals. <u>*Move only your right cymbal*</u> *and strike the left cymbal in an upward motion.*

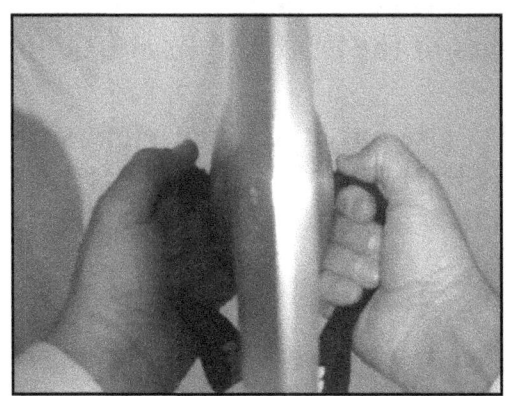
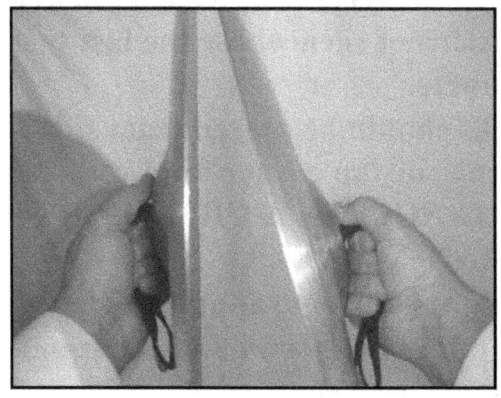

Rest cymbals on a trap table if available.

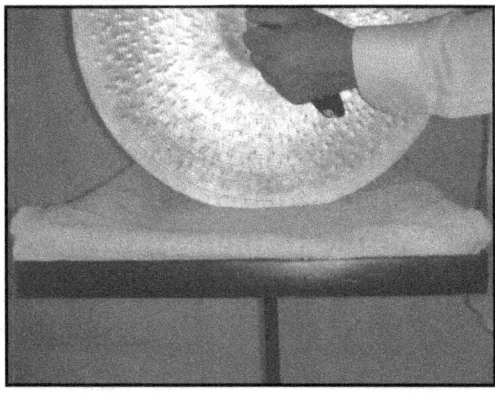

Lesson Twelve
Triangle

Description

The triangle is a metal instrument. Its name describes the shape of the instrument with one side of the triangle open. The triangle is *legato* and at times needs to be muffled. Please pay close attention to the proper way to hold the triangle and its striking areas.

Key Points

- The parts of a triangle are the triangle, triangle clip, and the beater.
- Your left hand holds the triangle and your right hand holds the triangle beater. Make sure the <u>pointed end of the triangle clip</u> faces the conductor.
- The most common beating spot is located on the lower right corner of the triangle, the opposite side of the open end.
- Since the triangle is a *legato* instrument that needs to be muffled for sections of silence, use the last two fingers of the left hand to muffle the triangle.
- Rolls should be played from side to side. Use only the lower right side corner or top corner for a roll. **NEVER ROLL ALL THREE SIDES OF A TRIANGLE IN A CIRCULAR MOTION – THIS IS CALLED THE "DINNER CALL".**
- Hold the triangle approximately eye level.
- Clip the triangle on a music stand and use two beaters when playing complicated rhythms.

Questions

1. What hand do you use to hold the triangle? _____
2. What hand do you use to strike the triangle? _____
3. Where do you strike the triangle? _____
4. How do you roll the triangle, side to side or all three sides in a circular motion? _____
5. When do you need to clip the triangle on the music stand? _____
6. How high do you hold the triangle? _____

IMITATE WHAT YOU SEE

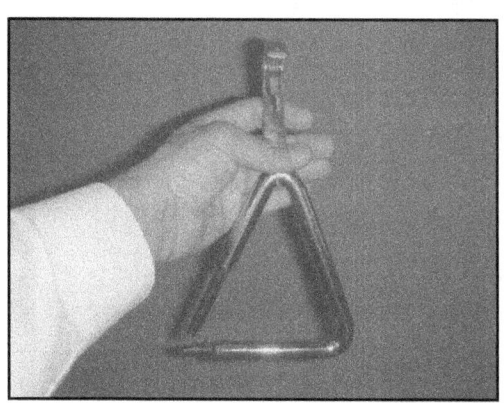

Left hand position

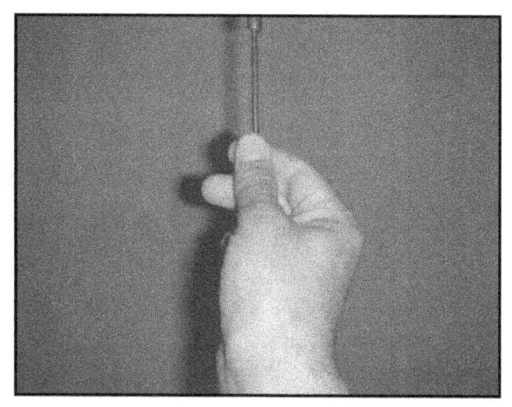

Right hand position (French Grip)

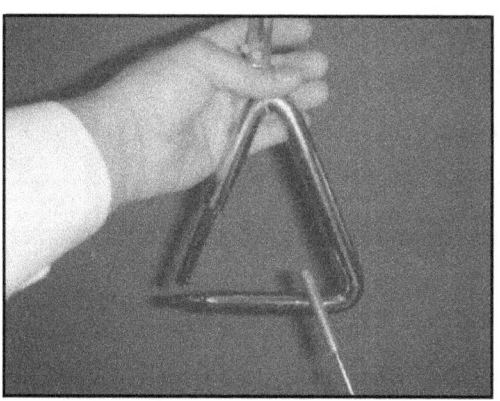

Hold triangle eye level. Open end of triangle is on the left side. Striking area is on the right side.

Playing complicated rhythms – clip triangle on the stand.

Lesson Thirteen
Tambourine

Description

The tambourine is a single headed drum that has jingle disks fitted around the rim. Striking the head or rim with your hand or shaking the tambourine creates its sound. It is an instrument that has been used in every style of music from classical music to gospel music. Pay attention to the proper way to hold a tambourine when playing rhythms.

Key Points

- Hold the tambourine in your left hand. Make sure your thumb is placed on top of the tambourine head.
- Keep the tambourine completely still and strike the tambourine with your right hand.
- Use your first three fingers of the right hand when playing soft and <u>play at the edge of the tambourine</u>.
- Use your fist of the right hand when playing loud.
- When playing a roll, shake the tambourine side to side.

Questions

1. In which hand do you hold the tambourine?
   _____
2. Which hand do you use to strike the tambourine?
   _____
3. When playing loud, do you use your fingers or fist?
   _____
4. When playing soft, do you use your fingers or fist?
   _____
5. How do you play a roll?
   _____

IMITATE WHAT YOU SEE

 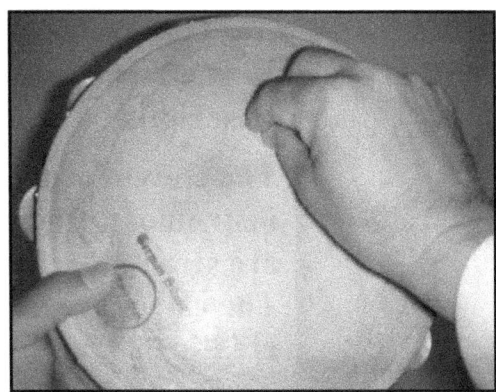

Use three fingers for playing soft "piano". Play at the edge of the tambourine.

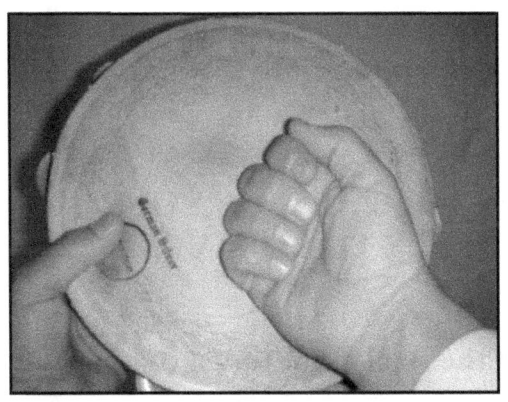 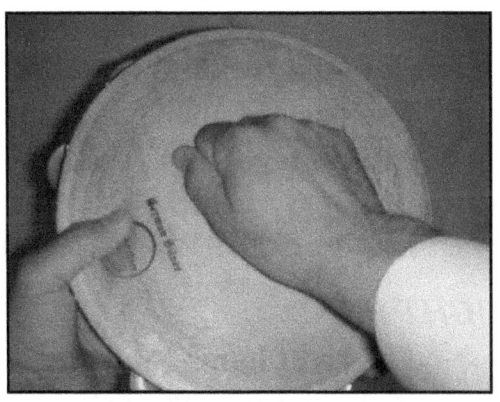

Use your fist when playing loud "forte".

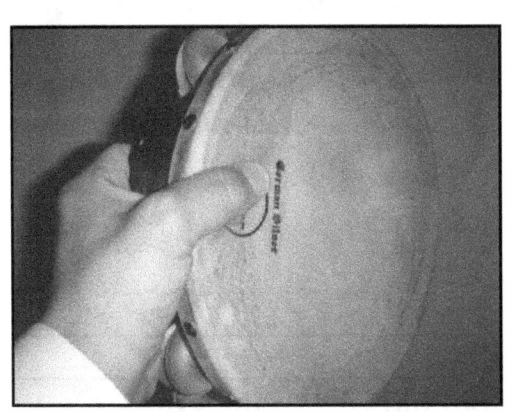

Hold the tambourine with your left hand on the open area of the tambourine. <u>Keep your thumb on top of the tambourine head.</u>

Lesson Fourteen
Claves

Description

The claves (pronounced *CLAH* - vays) are a Latin instrument. They are a pair of short wood sticks that are struck together to create a high - pitched sound. The claves are an extremely important instrument in creating a traditional Latin feel.

Key Points

LEFT HAND
- Cup your left hand and hold the clave with your finger tips. (see photo) <u>This creates a maximum amount of vibration.</u>
- The back of your hand is parallel to the ground and your palm is facing up.
- DO NOT HOLD THE CLAVE IN THE PALM OF YOUR LEFT HAND WHICH WILL MUFFLE THE CLAVE.

RIGHT HAND
- The right hand holds the clave at the back end, like a drum stick, and is used to strike the clave in your left hand.
- *Reminder* - Hold the claves loosely to create the maximum amount of vibration.

Questions

1. Which hand holds the clave that is struck? _____
2. Which hand holds the striking clave? _____
3. Do you hold the claves tightly or loosely? _____
4. Should you hold the back of your left hand parallel to the ground? _____
5. Why should you cup your left hand when holding the clave? _____

IMITATE WHAT YOU SEE

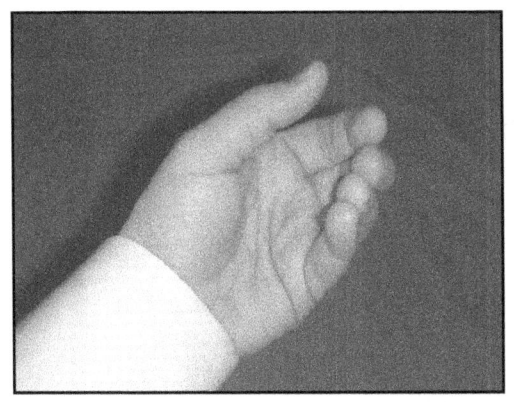

Cup your left hand.

Hold the clave with your finger tips.

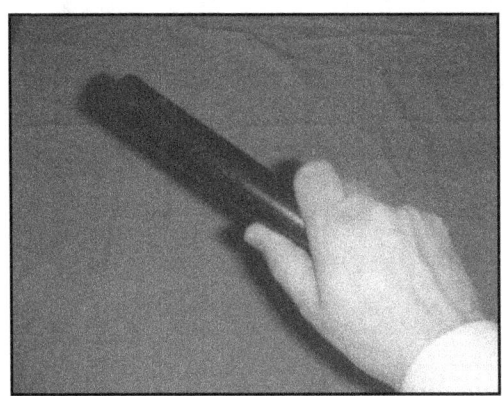

Your right hand holds the back end of the clave and strikes the left clave.

Lesson Fifteen
Maracas

Description

The Maracas are also a Latin instrument. They are a hand held instrument made from a gourd filled with beads. Its sound is created by shaking them and they're always played in pairs. It is difficult to play precise rhythms with this unique instrument. In Latin music the maracas keep the driving pulse.

Key Points

- Keep your wrist straight when playing rhythm. **MARACAS ARE THE ONLY PERCUSSION INSTRUMENT YOU <u>NEVER</u> USE YOUR WRIST. ONLY USE YOUR ARMS.**
- Be careful to keep the maracas still when you are not playing. The maracas will create sound. Remain completely still.
- Use the American grip when playing the maracas.

Questions

1. Which grip do you use when playing the maracas - French, German or American grip?
   _____
2. What should you do when you are holding the maracas and you have sections of rests?
   _____
3. True or False – Maracas are the only percussion instrument you never use your wrist, only your arms.
   _____

IMITATE WHAT YOU SEE

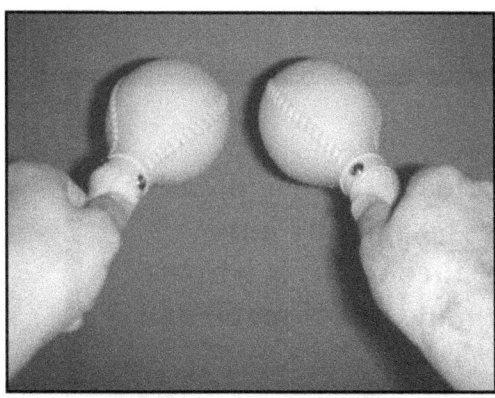

Use only your arms when playing rhythm. Never use your wrist.

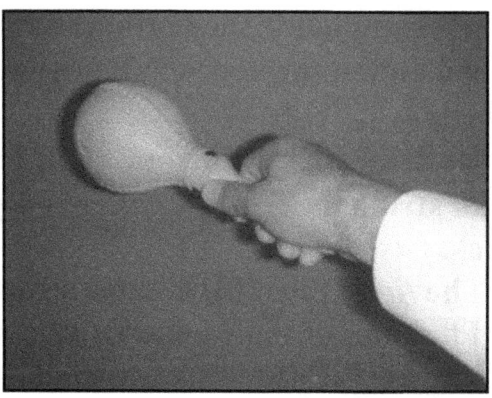

Use American grip when holding the maracas.

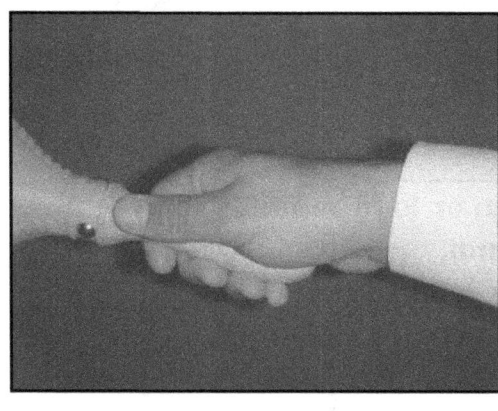

Keep your wrist straight when playing rhythms.

Lesson Sixteen
Cowbell

Description

The cowbell is a Latin American instrument. It is extremely popular in rock music and Latin music. The cowbell was originally hung around a cow's neck so herdsman could locate them. This is why we give this instrument its name "cowbell". It is made out of metal and struck with a drumstick.

Key Points

- Hold the cowbell with your left hand.
  Your left hand holds the bottom of the cowbell.
- The open end of the cowbell, known as the *mouth*, faces the opposite side of your body.
- Hold the drumstick with your right hand.
- You can strike the cowbell with the tip of the stick, shaft, or the back end of the stick. (see photo)
    1. The *tip* of the stick creates a soft sound.
    2. The *shaft* of the stick creates a medium sound.
    3. The *back* of the stick creates a loud sound.
- You can strike the cowbell in two areas.
    1. Strike the center of the cowbell for a high pitch tone.
    2. Strike the mouth of the cowbell for a low pitch tone.

Questions

1. Which hand holds the cowbell? _____
2. Which hand holds the drum stick? _____
3. The tip of the stick creates a soft, medium, or loud sound? _____
4. The shaft of the stick creates a soft, medium, or loud sound? _____
5. The back end of the stick creates a soft or loud sound? _____
6. Which part of the cowbell do you strike to create a high pitch tone?
   _____
7. Which part of the cowbell do you strike to create a low pitch tone?
   _____

IMITATE WHAT YOU SEE

The tip of the stick strikes the center of the cowbell.

The shaft of the stick strikes the mouth of the cowbell.

Use the back end of the stick to create a louder sound.

Lesson Seventeen
Temple Blocks

Description

The temple blocks originated in China, Japan, and Korea and were used for religious ceremonies. They are hollow wooden blocks of various sizes, which create tones from high to low. The sound of a temple block is similar to the sound of a wood block. Many school bands are using granite blocks that are more durable for beginning percussionists. Temple blocks are the perfect instrument to demonstrate the importance of proper mallet choice. Pay close attention to the exercise called "mallet choice" below.

Key Points

- For the best tone on the temple blocks, choose from your mallet list yarn mallets for proper sound.
- *Exception* - If you have a pair of hard rubber marimba mallets, they are the perfect temple blocks mallets even though they're not on your supply list.
- Be careful using xylophone mallets, it could damage the instrument.
- Do the mallet choice-playing exercise.

Mallet Choice Exercise

Exercise: Play one note with a drumstick, xylophone mallet, and a yarn mallet. Which mallet creates a core sound? You will notice the yarn mallet will create an amazing core sound. (Hard rubber marimba mallets are the best if available.)

Questions

1. Which mallets on your supply list create the best sound? _____
2. What mallets could you use if you own a pair? _____
3. Should you use drumsticks? _____
4. What mallets should you never use? _____

IMITATE WHAT YOU SEE

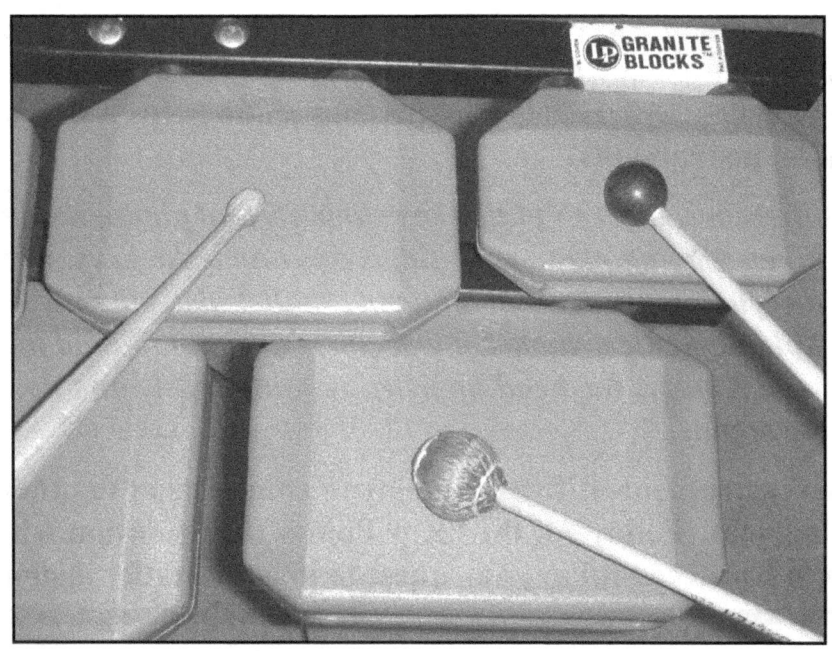

Play the Temple Blocks with a drum stick, xylophone mallet, and yarn mallet. You will notice the yarn mallet gives the temple blocks the best tone quality.

Lesson Eighteen A
Mallet Instruments

Description

"Mallet instruments" is a term used to describe the marimba, xylophone, bells, and vibraphone. These instruments have wooden or metal bars tuned to a chromatic scale, and are played with mallets. They originated in Africa, but Europeans modified them to look like a piano "keyboard". This is why playing piano helps a percussionist make the transition to mallet instruments.

There is one major difference between mallet instruments and piano, the inability to use the <u>sense of touch</u>. When playing piano your fingertips touch the keys, which allow your eyes to stay focused on reading music. When playing mallet instruments, the inability to feel the bars, due to holding mallets, makes it extremely difficult to read music. This is why a young percussionist moves his head up when reading music and down at the bars to find the correct note to play.

If you find the mallet instruments difficult to play in comparison to other percussion instruments, this is normal. Follow all the "Key Points" information which will give you a better chance to be successful in your quest to master mallet instruments.

Key Points

To create a great tone on a mallet instrument, you need to determine the correct mallet to use. There are many mallets to choose from, but use these guidelines to make your choice.

> To understand mallet choice, you need to understand which instrument has the hardest bars.
>
> *From hardest to softest:*
> 1. Bells (metal) have the hardest bars.
> 2. Xylophone has the hardest (wood) bars.
> 3. Marimba (wood) and vibraphone (metal) are equal.
> 4. Chimes (metal) are a unique instrument, struck with only a chime mallet. Never use sticks or xylophone mallets on chimes.
>
> BASIC RULE: <u>You can use a softer mallet on a harder instrument but never a harder mallet on a softer instrument</u>. If you use the wrong mallet, you can damage the instrument. For example: you can use a marimba mallet on a xylophone but never a xylophone mallet on a marimba or use a xylophone mallet on bells but never a <u>bell brass mallet</u> on a xylophone.

Mallet Choice

When purchased, mallets are labeled on the back of the package with the recommended instrument. Also, the label of the mallets is engraved on the side of the handles. The choice of mallets in *"Lesson One, Sticks and Mallets"* is very specific, but below are additional mallets that are not on the list.

Bells – Use brass, acrylic, or hard rubber mallets.

Xylophone – Use acrylic or hard rubber mallets.
You may choose one set of mallets for bells and xylophone. They will be labeled as bell /xylo mallets or use hard xylophone mallets. Never use yarn mallets (too soft) or brass mallets (too hard) on the xylophone.

Marimba – Yarn mallets or rubber mallets. *Never use xylophone mallets or drum sticks on the marimba. They will damage the bars.*

Vibraphone – Yarn mallets or cord mallets. I recommend yarn mallets for marimba and vibraphone. *Never use rubber mallets on the vibraphone. These mallets will create a poor tone quality.*

Chimes – Unique mallet choice – Chime mallets are shaped like a hammer. Only use chime mallets.

Questions

1. What mallets are recommended for xylophone and bells? _____
2. Should you use yarn mallets on a xylophone? _____
3. What mallets are recommended for marimba and vibraphone? _____
4. What would happen to the bars of a marimba if you use xylophone mallets or drum sticks? _____
5. What do chime mallets look like? _____
6. Is this statement true or false? You can always use soft mallets on hard bar instruments and it will never damage the bars. _____

Lesson Eighteen B
Mallet Instruments

Key Points

- Always strike (play) the *lower bars* in the center and over the resonators. The *top bars* can be played in the center or at the edge of the bar.
- Never strike the bar over the ropes called the *nodes*.
- Place left mallet above right mallet over bars. (see photo)
- Always keep your head still and only move your eyes when looking from your music to the instrument. This will keep you from losing your place in the music.
- Understand which instrument is a *legato* instrument (need to muffle to shorten tone) and which instrument is a *staccato* instrument (need to roll to sustain tone).

    1. Bells are legato. Muffle with your fingertips in measures of rest.
    2. Xylophone is a staccato instrument. Roll to sustain sound.
    3. Marimba is a staccato instrument. Roll to sustain sound.
    4. Vibraphone can be both a *legato* and *staccato* instrument. Sustain tones or muffle the bars using the pedal. The vibraphone pedal functions like a piano pedal. When not using the pedal, roll the note to sustain the tone.

Questions
1. What area do you strike the lower bars?
   Over the _____.
2. What two areas can you strike the top bars?
   _____
3. Should your left mallet be above your right mallet when playing? Yes or No_____
4. Which two mallet instruments do you need to roll in order to sustain sound? _____
5. Never strike the top bars over the _____.

IMITATE WHAT YOU SEE

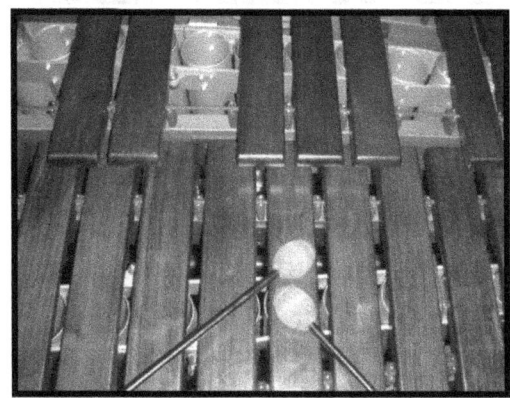

LOWER BARS - *Keep left mallet above the right mallet. Mallets are over the resonators.*

TOP BARS – *Strike the bar at the edge and never over the rope.*

TOP BARS - *Strike the bar over the resonators when time allows.*

Lesson Nineteen A
Timpani

Description

The timpani, also known as kettledrums, are the most used percussion instrument in the band and orchestra. It is a single head drum. The shell is hemispherical in shape and made of copper or fiberglass. It is tuned by adjusting the tension of the drum head with a pedal. The unique shell makes it important to understand where the proper beating spot is located. Each timpani is tuned to an exact pitch.

Key Points

- Place mallets close together approximately three inches from the rim of the timpani. *Never play in the center.* This is a dead spot on the timpani head.
- Use only timpani (felt) mallets; never use drumsticks. They will damage the timpani head.
- Allow the mallets to naturally bounce off the timpani head. Think of pulling the sound out of the drum, not playing into the drum.
- When playing a drum roll, hold the mallets apart. Always play a single stroke roll (r,l,r,l). Never use a double stroke roll (rr,ll,rr,ll).
- The timpani is a legato instrument. You need to muffle the timpani head with your fingertips after playing in measures of silence.
- To tune the timpani, push the pedal down (toe down) to raise the pitch. Push heel down to lower the pitch. NEVER PLAY WITH THE PEDAL. IT CAN BREAK DUE TO MISUSE.

Questions

1. How many inches from the rim is the playing area on the head? _____
2. Should the mallets be separated or close together when playing rhythm? _____
3. Should the mallets be separated or close together when playing a roll? _____
4. When you raise the pitch on the timpani, do you push the pedal down with your heel or toe? _____
5. When you lower the pitch on timpani, do you push the pedal down with your heel or toe? _____
6. Do you play a single stroke roll (r, l, r, l) or a double stroke roll (rr, ll, rr, ll) on timpani when playing a roll? _____
7. Are timpani mallets made of yarn or felt? _____

IMITATE WHAT YOU SEE

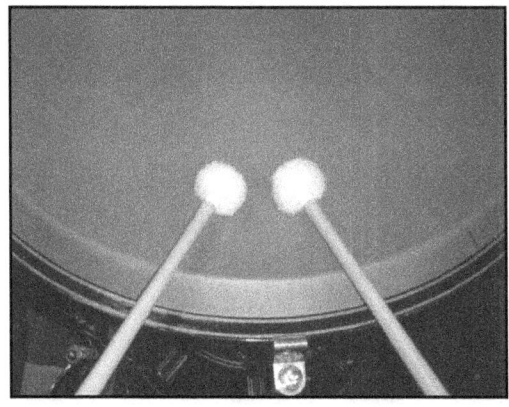

***When playing rhythm**, place mallets close together approximately three inches from the rim of the timpani.*

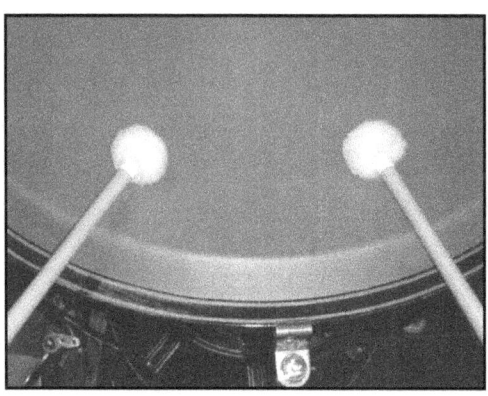

***When playing a roll**, separate timpani mallets approximately six inches apart and play a single stroke roll.*

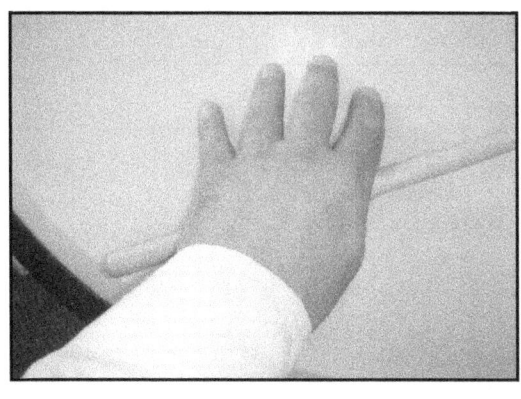

Muffle the timpani with your finger tips for measures of silence.

Lesson Nineteen B
Timpani Tuning

Description

Each timpani has a range of five diatonic notes, but a chromatic scale can be played on each drum. The notes below are common for a beginning percussionist. Each drum is identified by its size and has a specific range. Drum sizes – from your left side to your right side - biggest to the smallest - 32 inches, 29 inches, 26 inches, and 23 inches.

Key Points

These notes must be memorized to understand what timpani to use.

32" DRUM – D, E, F, G, A

29" DRUM – F, G, A, B flat, C

26" DRUM – B flat, C, D, E flat, F

23" DRUM – D, E, F, G, A

(The 32" drum and the 23" drum have the same notes but the 23" drum is an octave higher.)

Questions

1. What two drums can tune a B flat? _____
2. What two drums can tune a C? _____
3. What two drums have the same notes but an octave apart? _____
4. Write the five diatonic notes for each drum below.
   a. 32" ____, ____, ____, ____, ____
   b. 29" ____, ____, ____, ____, ____
   c. 26" ____, ____, ____, ____, ____
   d. 23" ____, ____, ____, ____, ____

Congratulations!

By completing "Percussion Guide for the Beginning Band Student", you are on your way to becoming a well-balanced percussionist.

To reinforce your percussion knowledge, continue with the series "Percussion Guide's Student Assessment."

This assessment book is a playing and written assessment based on *key points* from the percussion guide.

Also, visit my website at *nickbackos.com.* This website has instruction videos for each lesson.

If you have any questions or feedback regarding the percussion guide, please email me at nickbackos@gmail.com.

Sincerely,
Nick Backos

Reinforce key points from the Percussion Guide by continuing with:

Percussion Guide's *Student Assessment*

Playing and Written Assessment

By Nick Backos

New Edition

**Students Growth Assessment
for the instruction book,**

Percussion Guide for the Beginning Band Student

www.ingramcontent.com/pod-product-compliance
Lightning Source LLC
Chambersburg PA
CBHW080351170426
43194CB00014B/2748